Embroidered Alp

Gail Lawther

SEARCH PRESS

First published in Great Britain 1991
Search Press Limited,
Wellwood, North Farm Road,
Tunbridge Wells, Kent TN2 3DR

Photography by Search Press Studios

Extra artwork provided by Christopher Lawther,
Lydia Knights and Julian Smith

Inspired by Sharon Perna, Graphique Needle Arts

ISBN 0 85532 652 2

Phototypeset by Scribe Design, 123 Watling Street,
Gillingham, Kent
Printed and bound by Times Publishing Group, Singapore.

Introduction

What do you think of when you picture embroidered alphabets? Samplers, probably; the little cross-stitch pictures and letters worked by young girls in the nineteenth century, to teach them their letters and how to sew in one task. As they sat, straight-backed, in their parlours or school-rooms, they probably didn't think embroidering alphabets was much fun – but it is! Today, lettering has become an art in itself; look around at billboards, Sunday supplements, television graphics and business stationery, and you'll see that designers are using unlimited imagination to create and reproduce beautiful letters, and embroidery is no exception. With such inspiration around us, and the rich and varied threads and materials that we have available today, embroidering letters can provide endless scope for our creativity.

Maybe you want to embroider a simple message to celebrate a special occasion – a marriage, birth, graduation or anniversary. Perhaps you want to do your own modern sampler, trying out different stitches, letterforms and colour combinations. Or perhaps you want to try embellishing simple letters to make a really ornate piece of textured embroidery. Whichever it is, this book will provide you with lots of ideas and inspiration, as well as many alphabets and individual letters for you to use and adapt.

As well as the alphabets in this book, look around you and in library books for inspiration from posters, magazines, and calligraphy. Start making your own adaptations, and you'll soon discover just how much of an art form embroidered lettering can be!

Materials

Very little initial expense is incurred when experimenting with embroidered lettering. Scraps of fabric need never be wasted and you can use up small lengths of thread to create very colourful effects.

Fabrics

Just about any fabric can be used for embroidered alphabets, but you'll find it easiest to start with firm cottons and evenweave fabrics. For square-stitch designs you can use evenweaves, canvas, or binca, which are all produced in different numbers of threads to the centimetre/inch and varying colours. Pale fabrics can be dyed with food colours or fabric dyes; these produce more subtle shades of background than some of the cruder ready-coloured ones available.

Threads

There are wonderful ranges of thread available for embroidery, and most of them are produced in a wide variety of colours and shades. The best threads to start with are stranded cottons; these come in skeins of six twisted strands, but fewer strands can be used for finer work. Coton à broder is a fine, shiny, twisted thread; coton perlé, or pearl cotton, is a thicker, even more shiny thread, available in several thicknesses.

Soft cotton is a thread with a matt finish; it is fairly thick, so is best used on canvas or binca, or in a large needle through a firm fabric. Silk threads are very fine and rather expensive, but look wonderful for delicate embroidery designs.

Other materials

You will need a range of ordinary needles – crewel embroidery and sharps are best because of their large eyes – as well as tapestry needles, which have rounded tips. You will also need large and small scissors, embroidery frames for keeping the work taut, a ruler, a selection of soft pencils, and a water-soluble pen for transferring your designs.

Plain paper and paper with a square grid, and a selection of coloured pencils or pens, will be useful for making your own charts and designs.

1 canvas
2 coloured binca
3 canvases and binca/aida/hardanger in different thread counts
4 plain papers for working out designs
5 squared papers for working out designs using square stitches
6 embroidery hoop
7 cotton and synthetic threads
8 coton perlé (pearl cotton)
9 stranded cottons
10 soft cottons
11 metallic threads
12 sewing needles
13 tapestry needles
14 pencil
15 water-erasable pen for marking fabric

Outline stitches

Outline stitches can be used to embroider round the edges of letters, or used on their own to represent fine letterforms (such as the alphabet on page 1). Very delicate outlines can be created by working stitches such as back stitch in fine threads; stronger outlines can be worked in stitches such as chain stitch, or whipped running stitch, or by using thick threads such as soft cotton.

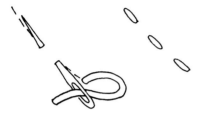

Running stitch

This is the most basic of all embroidery stitches. Bring the thread through to the front of the fabric on the outline to be stitched. Insert the needle a little way further along the line, and bring it out again slightly beyond that. This will produce a broken line of straight stitches.

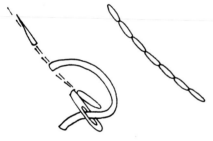

Back stitch

Form a running stitch from right to left, then bring the needle through to the front a little way beyond the first stitch. Insert the needle at the end of the first stitch and let it emerge a little way beyond the thread, and pull through. Continue in this way along the stitching line.

Split stitch

Make a small running stitch to begin, then bring the needle out to the front through the first stitch. Insert the needle a little further along the stitching line, and bring it out through the second stitch. Continue in this way along the stitching line.

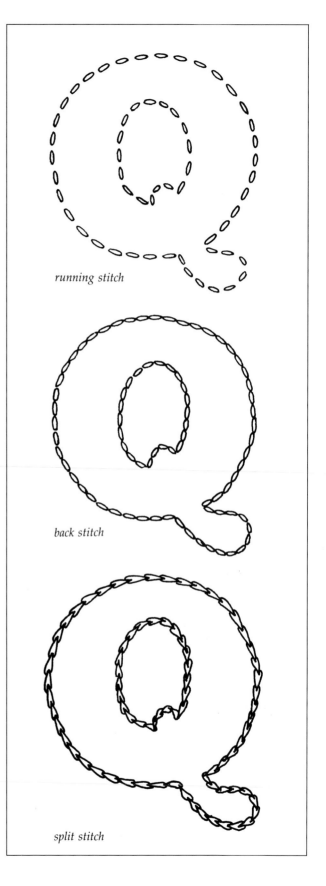

running stitch

back stitch

split stitch

Whipped running stitch

Work a line of running stitch round the stitching line. Then, using a contrasting thread, weave through the stitches from left to right and from right to left, without taking the needle through to the back of the fabric. Finish off the thread by taking it through to the back under the final stitch.

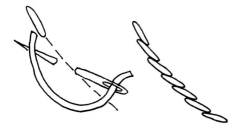

Stem stitch

Make a long running stitch along the stitching line, then bring the needle out halfway along the first stitch, just to one side of it. Insert the needle slightly further along the stitching line, and continue in the same way.

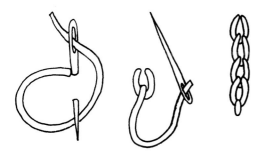

Chain stitch

With the thread at the front of the fabric, insert the needle where the thread emerges and bring it out slightly further down the stitching line. Pull the needle and thread through to form a chain link, and continue in the same way. Secure the final chain link with a tiny running stitch.

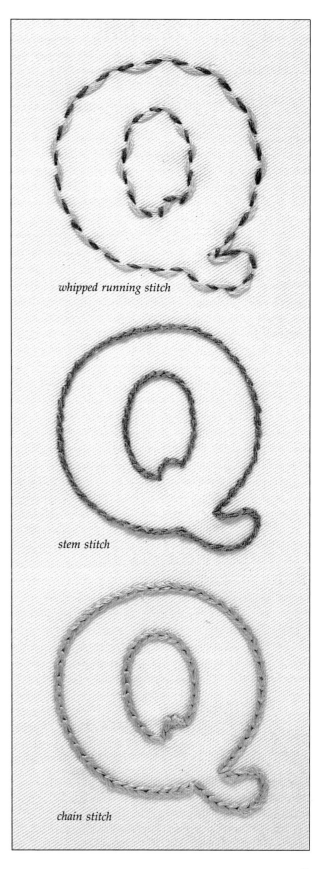

whipped running stitch

stem stitch

chain stitch

Filling stitches

If you are embroidering a thick letter, you may want to fill in the middle of the strokes with one of many filling stitches that have developed over the years. Filling stitches range from the simple to the very complex; six of the most straightforward variations are shown here.

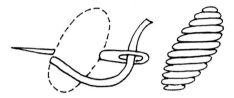

Satin stitch

Beginning at the widest point of the shape to be filled, bring the thread out on one side. Then take a stitch across the shape at the desired angle, bringing the needle tip out just next to your first stitch. Continue in this way until the shape is filled.

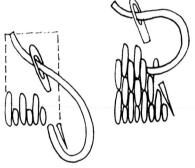

Long and short stitch

Beginning at the top or bottom of your shape, work a row of alternate long and short stitches. For each subsequent row work stitches of even lengths butting up to the previous row. End with a row of alternate long and short stitches to fill the shape.

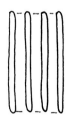

Criss-cross stitch

Begin by working a series of vertical, well-spaced satin stitches at regular intervals across the shape to be filled. Then work a series of horizontal stitches across the shape, weaving each one alternately over and under the vertical threads. Make sure that if you go under one thread with the first stitch you go over with the next.

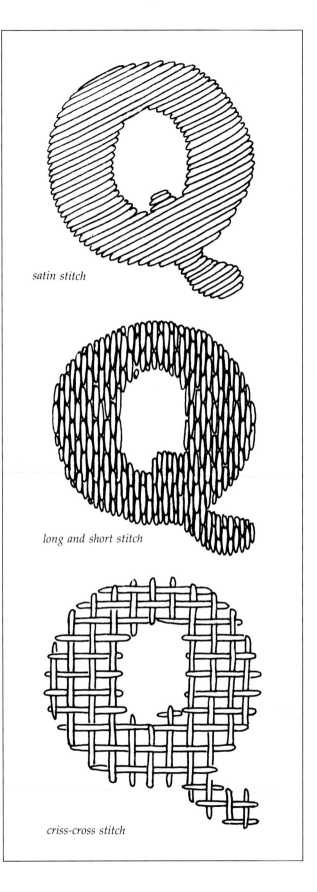

satin stitch

long and short stitch

criss-cross stitch

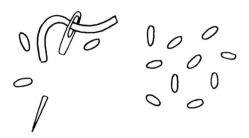

Seeding
Build up a series of tiny running stitches in the shape to be filled; these can either be worked at random, as here, or all worked in the same direction.

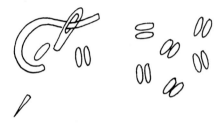

Double seeding
This stitch works in the same way as seeding, but the tiny running stitches are worked in parallel pairs.

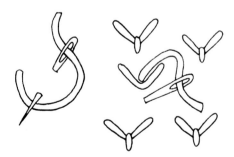

Fly stitch
Bring the thread out to the front of the fabric and insert the needle slightly to the right, pointing it diagonally downwards. Pull the needle and thread through, then take a tiny vertical stitch to secure the V shape. Use random scatterings of fly stitch to fill the shape.

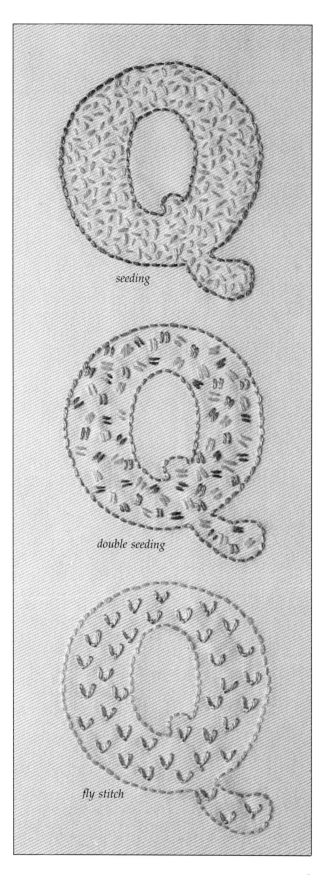

seeding

double seeding

fly stitch

Square stitches

We're all familiar with the cross stitch alphabets found on samplers, but if you're embroidering on evenweave fabric, canvas or binca you don't have to confine yourself just to cross stitch. All the stitches here are worked in regular blocks that can be built up into letterforms; if you're not using evenweave fabric, just draw a grid on your fabric first.

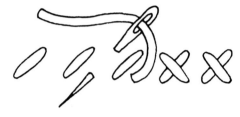

Cross stitch

This is the easiest square stitch to work. Make a series of regular diagonal stitches slanting in one direction, then work back along the row making stitches that cross the first ones.

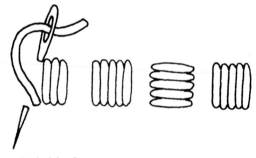

Satin stitch blocks

Satin stitch blocks use the same technique as ordinary satin stitch (see page 8), but are worked over a square of threads or fabric. You can use blocks of satin stitch worked in different directions to produce textured letters.

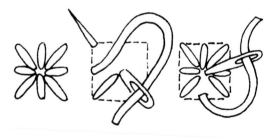

Algerian stitch

Strictly, this is a canvaswork stitch, but it can be used to stitch over any square. Eight stitches radiate from the centre of the square to its corners and halfway along each side.

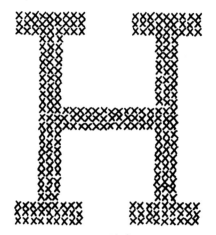

cross stitch

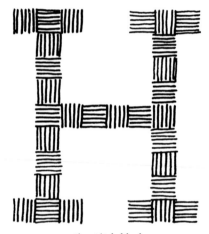

satin stitch blocks

Algerian stitch

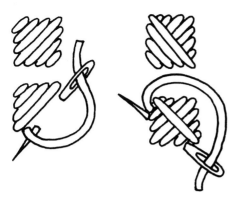

Cushion stitch

Cushion stitch is a block of satin stitch worked on the diagonal (left). In crossed cushion stitch (right), half the square is stitched over again in the opposite direction.

Rhodes stitch

This is like satin stitch worked in a wheel. Begin at any point on the edge of the square, and work a series of clockwise stitches across the shape until it is covered. (This stitch can also be used for circles.)

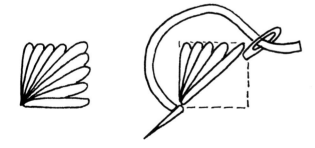

Fan stitch

The idea of fan stitch is similar to Algerian stitch, but here all the stitches radiate from one corner of the square. Begin with the upright stitch and move round clockwise to the horizontal stitch.

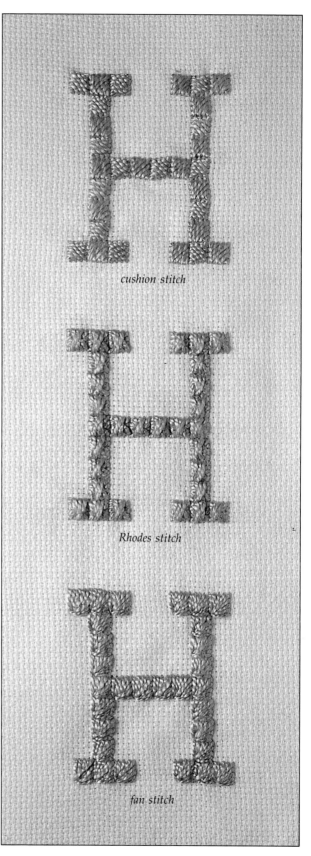

cushion stitch

Rhodes stitch

fan stitch

Basics of lettering

To embroider alphabets well you will need to develop an eye for the characteristics of different letterforms. Consistency is important; the letters in your alphabet need to look as though they belong together, so on these pages we'll take a quick look at some of the elements you need to be aware of as you turn letters into embroidery designs.

different types of lettering

Style
The style of an alphabet is the overall impression it gives. Is it old-fashioned, ornate, classical, ultra-modern, rigid, flowing, quirky, compact? The letters on the left are examples of many different styles.

ABCDEFGHIJKLM
NOPQRSTUVWXYZ

abcdefghijklmnopqrstuvwxyz

upper and lower case letters

Upper and lower case
Upper case letters, or capitals, are the ones we use to begin sentences or names. Lower case letters are sometimes simply called small letters.

ABC abc   **ABC** abc

ABC abc   **ABC** abc

body height

Body height
This is the height of the lower case letters; it may be very small compared with the height of the capitals, or it may be nearly the same. The illustrations show a variety of body heights against capitals of the same size.

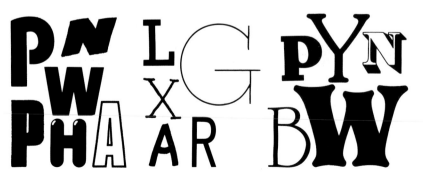

thin and thick ratio

Thick and thin ratio
Some alphabets have very thick (left) or very thin (centre) strokes throughout the letters; others have a combination of thick and thin strokes (right), as these examples show.

HHHH H

serifs and sans serif

Serifs

Serifs are the lines or swellings that appear at the ends of a letter's main strokes. Serifs can take many different forms (left); letterforms without serifs are called sans serif (right).

OOOO

stress

Stress

The stress of a letter is the angle of its thickest line; in a consistent alphabet, the stress will be the same throughout the letters. The examples here show 'Os' with the stress in different directions.

MMMM

bold and light

Bold and light

Bold alphabets are ones where the strokes are all quite thick; fine or light ones have thinner strokes throughout. Letters can be redrawn, to make them bolder or lighter.

uuuu

condensing and expanding

Condensing and expanding

If a letter is very narrow for its height, it is called condensed; if it is very wide it is called expanded. Letters can be condensed or expanded by redrawing them narrower or wider.

variations

Variations

There are endless different kinds of letterforms; for instance, look at all the different versions of one letter shown here. It's hard to believe that they all represent the same letter of the alphabet!

Transferring alphabet designs

There are various ways in which you can transfer your lettering design on to your fabric. If the fabric is fairly fine you will probably be able to trace a strong line through the fabric by putting the design underneath it; use a faint pencil line or a water-soluble embroidery pen for the tracing. If the fabric is thicker, laying it on a designers' light-box will help you to see through it so that you can trace the design underneath.

Using dressmakers' carbon paper is another way of transferring a design. Lay the carbon paper, carbon side down, on the right side of the fabric, and put the design on top, then trace over the lines of the design with a pencil. This will leave a carbon outline on the fabric.

If you want to use the same design several times you can make a reusable transfer by drawing with a special transfer pen; this can then be ironed on to the fabric in the traditional way. Remember that you will have to draw your transfer in *reverse* so that it appears on the fabric the right way round.

Enlarging and reducing

If you want to change the size of a letter, draw a grid of squares over it (above), then redraw the grid with the squares smaller (centre) or larger (below), and copy the lines of the letters as they appear on the original squares.

Drawing outlines

If you start off with a solid letter, you can turn it into an outline form just by drawing round the edges (left). If you want a thicker outline, you can draw the other border for it either outside (centre) or inside (right) the first line, to produce different results.

drawing outlines

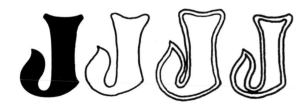

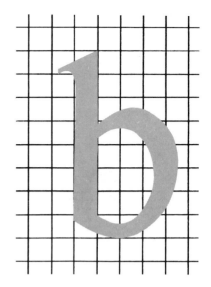

reducing

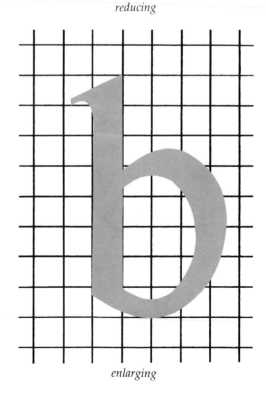

enlarging

Square-stitch to freehand

If you want to adapt a square-stitch letter for freestyle embroidery, simply smooth out the square edges of the design to make a pleasing curve.

Freehand to square-stitch

If you want to adapt a freestyle letter for square-stitch embroidery, draw or trace the letter on to graph paper. Then fill in the squares that most closely correspond to the shape of the letter, to give you a square-stitch chart.

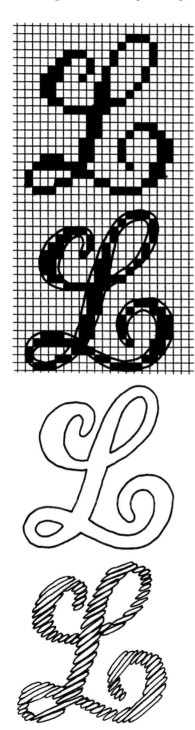

square-stitch to freehand

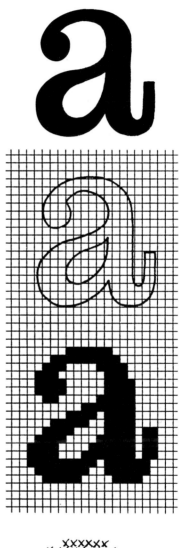

freehand to square-stitch

15

Alphabet 1

This extremely simple square-stitch alphabet could be used to make your own modern sampler to commemorate a special event. The upper and lower case letters are very straightforward, and numbers have been added as well, so that dates can be represented.

alphabet 1

Cross stitch in graduated shades of blue/green stranded cotton has been used to stitch
the alphabet, and a simple border has been added in the three colours. The top threads
of the cross stitch all slant in the same direction.

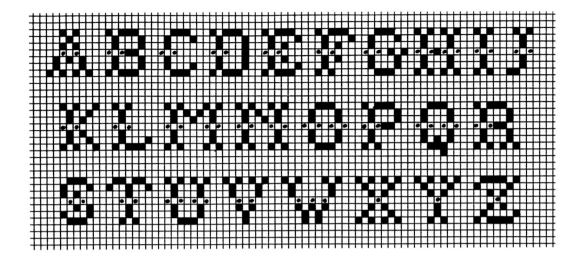

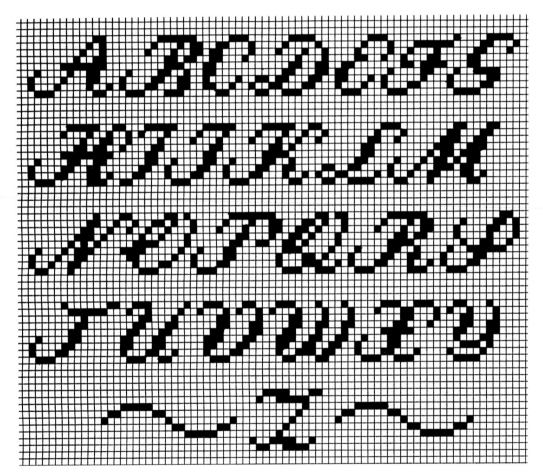

Alphabets 2 and 3

The top alphabet (2) is based on traditional sampler lettering, and is quite simple to do; each letter has a decorative square of stitches, and the ends of the strokes have pronged serifs.

The bottom alphabet (3) is based on an ornate Victorian cross stitch alphabet, full of decorative flourishes.

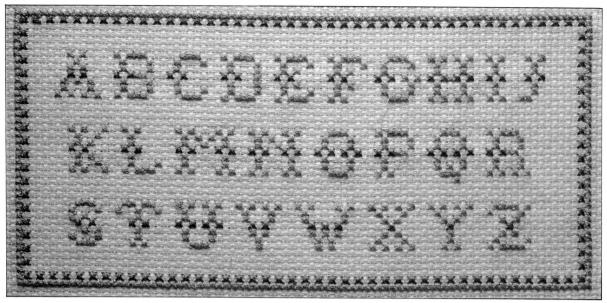

alphabet 2

alphabet 3

The binca for the top alphabet (2) has been dyed a pale pink, (see page 4), and the alphabet worked in cross stitch in two colours of stranded cotton. The bottom alphabet (3) is worked in coton perlé on canvas, using Rhodes stitch.

19

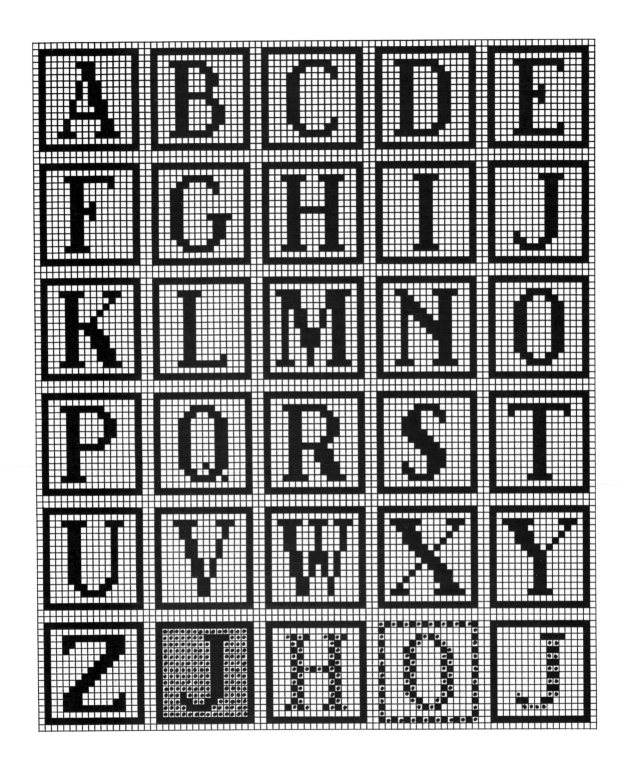

Alphabet 4

This attractive alphabet is a sampler form based on traditional Roman capital letters. The letters have simple serifs at the ends of the main strokes, and each letter is enclosed in its own 16-stitch square box.

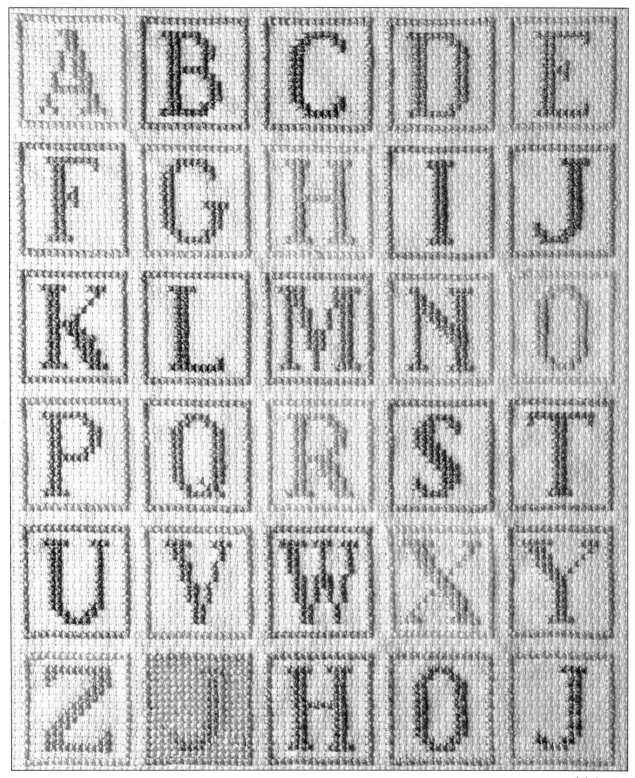

alphabet 4

The alphabet has been stitched in pastel stranded cottons, with each box a lighter shade of the coloured letter it contains. The final four letters show ways of varying the colour combinations.

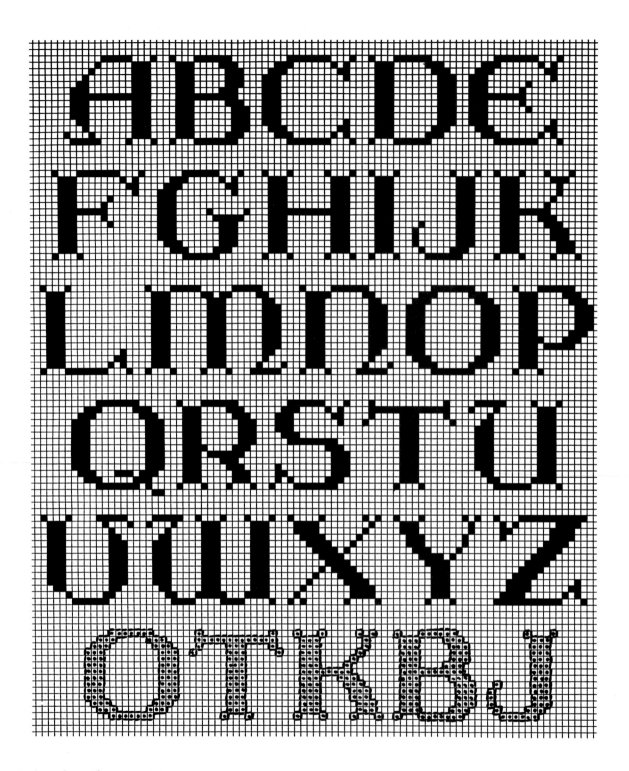

Alphabet 5

Uncial and half-uncial letterforms of the 8th–10th century are the inspiration for this square-stitch alphabet. Note the very thick main strokes and the fine curved serifs at the ends. The final line shows the principle of edging the letters with straight lines of back stitch.

22

alphabet 5

The rows of the alphabet have been embroidered in graduating shades of beige and brown stranded cotton, with a thin gold lurex thread used in the needle at the same time. Each letter in the bottom line has been embroidered in gold lurex thread and dark brown soft cotton.

23

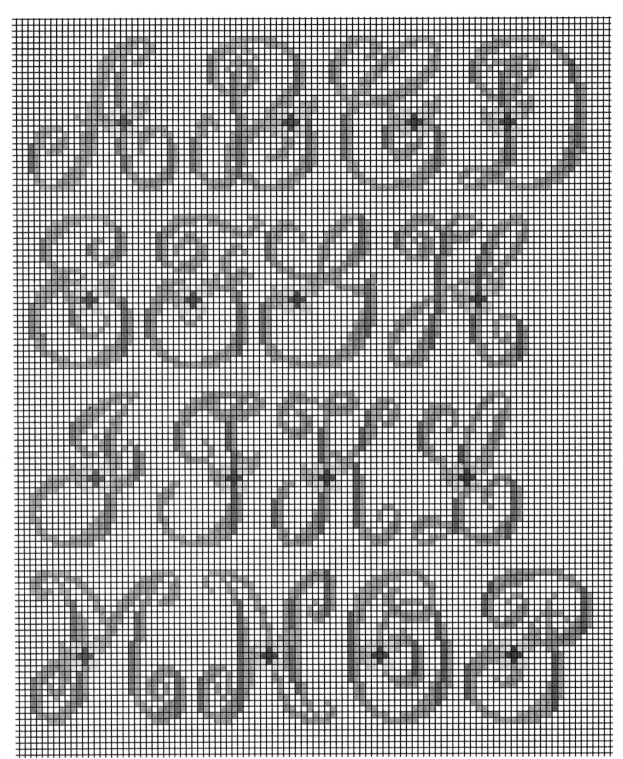

Alphabet 6

Highly ornate, florid alphabets were loved by the Victorians, and this square-stitch alphabet is in that style. Each letter is formed in two shades of blue and has a simple flower and leaf motif inserted in the centre.

24

alphabet 6

The final four letters show a different colour combination that could be used for the letters and flowers. Also shown are small motifs that could be substituted for the flower.

ABCDE
FGHIJK
LMNOP
QRSTUV
WXYZ

Alphabet 7

Versal alphabets were used as capital letters on illuminated manuscripts in the middle ages, and are the inspiration for this alphabet. All the main strokes are waisted – they swell outwards at the ends – and are capped by long, thin, curved cross-strokes.

alphabet 7

Only four colours of stranded cotton have been used to embroider the versal alphabet,
but they show the enormous variety of ways that simple letters can be embroidered,
from a basic running stitch outline to a cross stitch letter in four graduated shades.

abcdefg
hijklmn
opqrstu
vwxyz

Alphabet 8

Italic handwriting is a good source of inspiration for
embroidered letters, as this alphabet shows. The
stress of the letters is diagonal and there are no
rounded curves; instead, the letters form a point at
the top and lower edge.

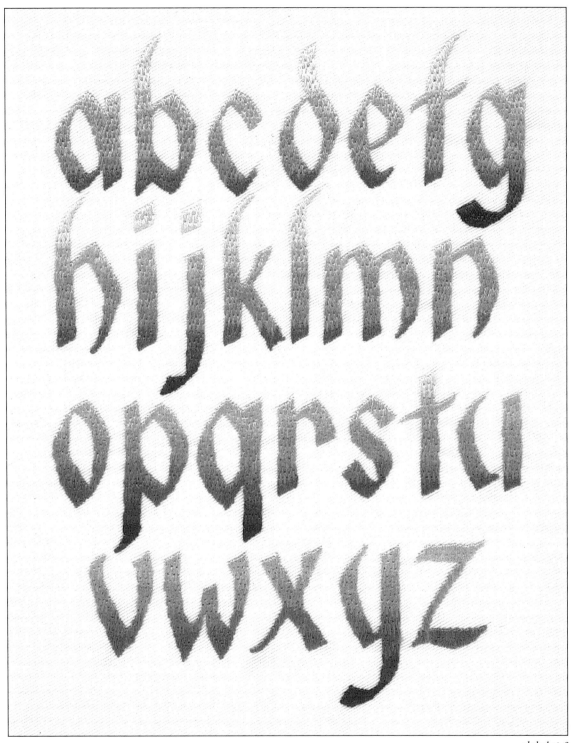

alphabet 8

Ten graduated shades of blue stranded cotton have been used to embroider the italic letterform. Two strands of each colour were used so that the stitches were fine, and the whole alphabet was worked in long and short stitch (see page 8).

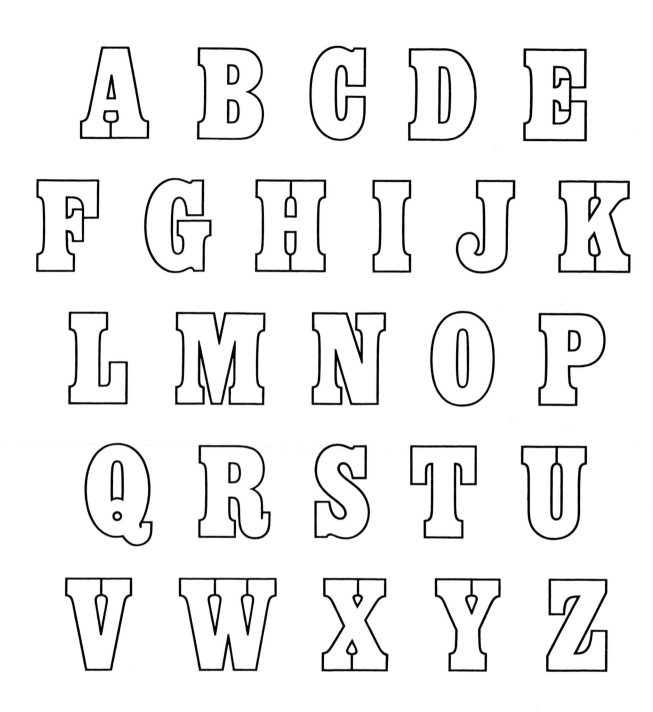

Alphabet 9

Letterforms with large, slab-like serifs are known as Egyptian style letters; this one is based on a typeface called Egyptian Outline. All the strokes are thick, and the serifs are large slabs, attached to the main strokes with curves.

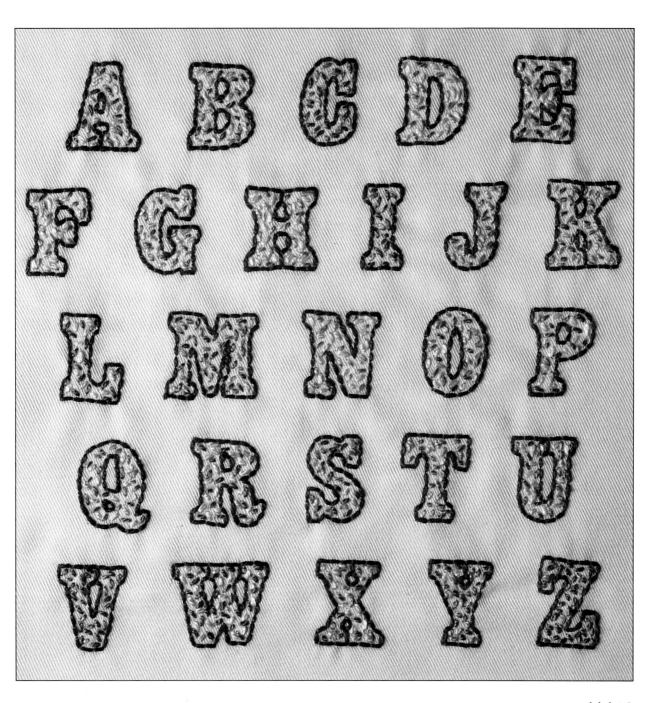

alphabet 9

The alphabet has been embroidered in outline, using cerise coton perlé and working in back stitch. Each letter has been filled in with random seeding, (see page 9), using a variegated pink thread.

ABCDE
FGHIJK
LMNOP
QRSTU
VWXYZ

Alphabet 10

This modern reworking of a classical Roman style is based on a typeface called Souvenir Light. The strokes are fine and delicate, and finish in small serifs with rounded edges.

ABCDE
FGHIJK
LMNOP
QRSTU
VWXYZ

Thirteen different bright colours of stranded cotton have been used to embroider the alphabet, with two letters worked in each colour. The letters were embroidered in satin stitch, worked at a slant.

ABCDE
FGHIJK
LMNOP
QRSTU
VWXYZ

Alphabet 11

Frankfurter is the name of this bold, fat, sans serif typeface. Each letter is made up of thick strokes with rounded tips; all the strokes of the letters are virtually the same width, and there is no noticeable stress.

34

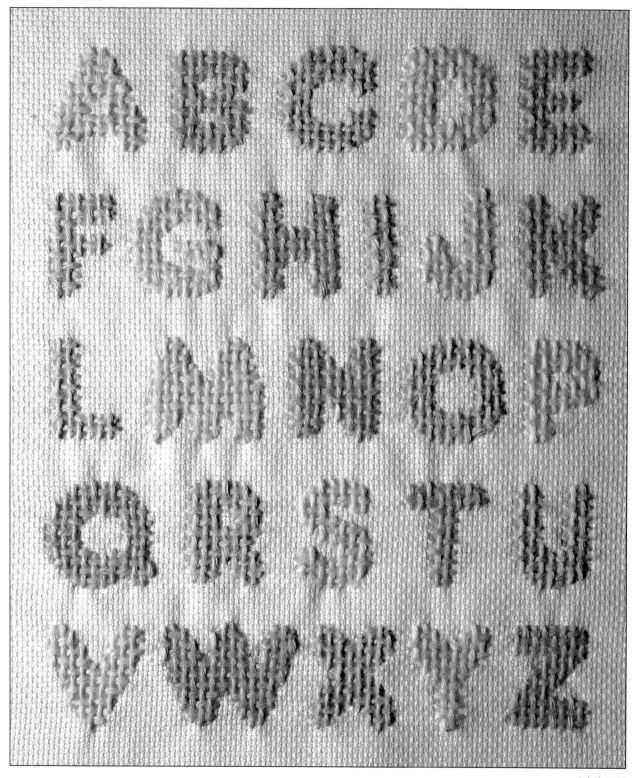

Criss-cross stitch, (see page 8), in three pastel shades of soft cotton has been used to embroider the alphabet; no outline stitch was used, as the pattern made by the criss-cross stitch defines the shape sufficiently.

Alphabet 12

Thick, double, overlapping lines were used to create this quirky alphabet. The letterforms are kept as simple as possible, and placing each letter at a different angle adds to the feeling of asymmetry.

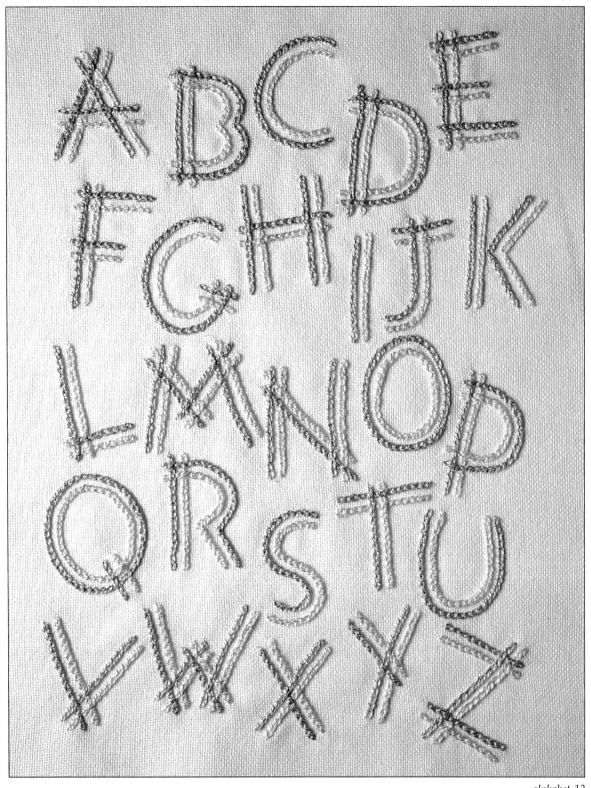

alphabet 12

Chain stitch in two different colours of stranded cotton was used for the embroidery,
keeping the blue line to the left throughout and overlapping the yellow with blue where
the two colours meet.

Machine embroidery

Using a sewing machine for stitching letterforms is one of the most effective types of machine embroidery; the controls of the machine keep the widths and lengths of the stitches regular, which produces good consistent letters.

Some machines do all kinds of exotic embroidery stitches – including, on some models, an imitation cross stitch – but all the letters shown here can be produced with a machine that simply does straight stitch and zigzag. Use the zigzag facility at the closest stitch-length setting to produce lines of satin stitch.

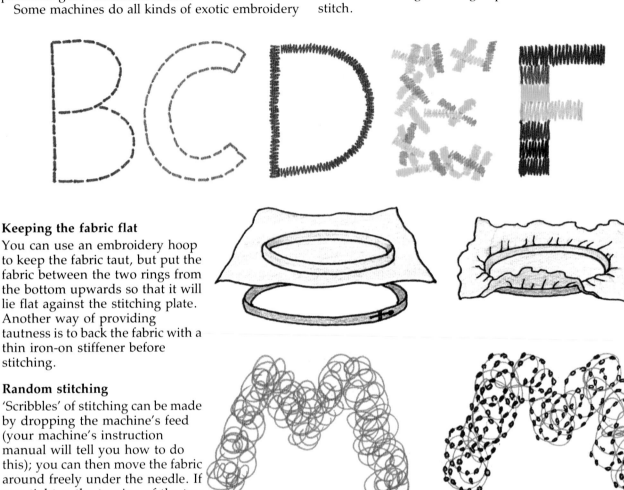

Keeping the fabric flat

You can use an embroidery hoop to keep the fabric taut, but put the fabric between the two rings from the bottom upwards so that it will lie flat against the stitching plate. Another way of providing tautness is to back the fabric with a thin iron-on stiffener before stitching.

Random stitching

'Scribbles' of stitching can be made by dropping the machine's feed (your machine's instruction manual will tell you how to do this); you can then move the fabric around freely under the needle. If you tighten the tension of the top thread and use a contrasting thread in the bobbin, the bobbin thread will appear as loops of colour on the surface.

Appliqué

Machine stitching is ideal for appliquéing letters in different fabrics. To prevent fraying, cut the letters out of fabric backed with iron-on stiffener and stitch to the backing fabric, using zigzag or satin stitch.

38

These machine-embroidered letters have been placed at random and worked in four shades of glitter yarn, plus gold.

Embellishing letters

Letters can be enhanced in countless very simple ways just by adding different outlines, or shadows of varying thicknesses, by working the letter in dots or stripes, or by varying colour combinations. These pages show just some of the numerous variations that can easily be worked on one plain letter.

Combining letters

There are many ways in which letters can be combined to make words, names, logos, or monograms. The letters can be put in boxes, arranged in different ways, put on top of one another, intertwined, linked through different shades of one colour or a colour progression, and combined within borders and shapes. These two pages show a few of the many ways of combining individual letters.

Abstract letters

Once you have got used to the principles of regular letterforms, you can vary the basic forms by making them asymmetric or irregular. Experimenting with brushes, crayons and calligraphic pens will help you form free, abstract shapes and textures which can then be rendered in embroidery; these two pages show a few examples of asymmetric forms.

Complex letters

When your lettering is confident, there is no limit to the ornate and bizarre letters that you can design for embroidery! You can imitate different effects, such as flowers or stained glass, or simply experiment endlessly with patterns, textures and colour combinations – as these pages show.

Illumination

The principle of illumination is to take a basic letterform and add more and more ornamentation to it in different colours. The three drawings below show how a basic versal letter 'G' (Fig a) had outlines, see Fig b, and textures, see Fig c, added to produce the final sketch for the finished embroidery. Gold beads, gold thread and rich, jewel-like colours give an appearance of opulence.

fig a *fig b* *fig c*